More Than Enough

APRIL WILLIAMS

ISBN 979-8-88751-500-7 (paperback)
ISBN 979-8-88751-501-4 (digital)

Copyright © 2022 by April Williams

All rights reserved. No part of this publication may be reproduced, distributed, or transmitted in any form or by any means, including photocopying, recording, or other electronic or mechanical methods without the prior written permission of the publisher. For permission requests, solicit the publisher via the address below.

Christian Faith Publishing
832 Park Avenue
Meadville, PA 16335
www.christianfaithpublishing.com

Printed in the United States of America

INTRODUCTION

The message that I hope to share with you through *More Than Enough* is one that was given to me by the Holy Spirit during a time in which I felt like I was everything but enough, a time where I felt like I was everything but what God told me I was. I was coming from a place where I had verbally been told that I was not enough, and God then came to me and told me, "I know what you were told. I know what you heard from man, but hear what I'm telling you through My Word. You are fearfully and wonderfully made (Psalm 139:14). You are more than enough." Then He told me to write it.

I want everyone reading this to know that I wrote this book to empower, to encourage, and to birth the hidden gifts and anointing in all who read it. I wrote this book for anyone, male or female, who may be like me and have found themselves in moments of self-doubt, for anyone who may be struggling to believe, and for anyone who may have been knocked down by people, opportunities, or failed attempts. My prayer for you as you read this book is that it will change your life for the better and that it will help you to view yourself the same way God views you. Not what people say, not what social media says, and not what you say but what God says about who you are.

As you read this book, I want you to read it with an open mind. Let the Word of God touch your heart and mind as you read. This book is about breaking down the boundaries, walls, and barriers that keep us from being all that God has called us to be. It's time for God's children to live out loud and to no longer be overruled by the world that tells us how we should live our lives. My prayer is that as you read this book, it will change your view of yourself and those around you. My prayer is that it will equip you with the knowledge to withstand and identify the tricks of the enemy and to be able to come out victorious because you have taken the time to evaluate what God's Word says about who you are.

After reading this book, I want for us as believers to no longer become satisfied with just enough ever again, but I want us to strive for more than enough in everything we set our minds toward because we are indeed more than enough, and it's time we start living like it. If you are like me and you're tired of complacency and want to see more of God in your life, this book is for you. Allow it to challenge, check, and change you so that you can be all that God has called you to be.

CHAPTER 1

There Is Power in Your Words

"There is power in your words." I know you have heard this phrase so many times, and it sounds cliché, but it is true, and it's important for you to get this in your spirit. Proverbs 18:21 tells us that death and life are in the power of the tongue. Meaning, the words that you speak literally have the ability to either birth something or the ability to kill something. So why don't we speak life into our situations more often if we know that what we say has power?

In Genesis 1:3, when God was creating the world, He spoke the words, "Let there be light," and the Bible says there was light. There are two things to take note of here. First, God spoke something and immediately it came to pass. I believe that it came to pass because God *knew* that all He had to do was to speak it. He told us that the power is in our tongue. Not only was God aware of the power of His words, He didn't just know that there was power in His words but secondly, He *believed* it. He even had faith in knowing that He is God and that He can make all things come to pass. God knew and He believed, so why is it that we as children of this Almighty, all-powerful God still struggle with knowing the true power of our words?

I want to answer this question by saying that maybe for most of us, we know what the Word says about our words, but we as humans lack the faith to believe that our words can hold so much weight. We get stuck on the idea of who we are or what we've done that we take the power off our own lives by not even activating it. We have allowed the saying itself to lose its power because maybe we don't really believe it. I want to stop here because if we don't believe in the power of our words, it's simply because we lack the faith to believe. And this very reason may be why we as believers and followers of Christ are so careless with how we speak over our own lives and the lives of others around us.

The power goes both ways

I think we would take our words more serious if we really take the time to dissect what Proverbs 18:21 is saying to us. The Word says that the power of *life* and *death* is in our tongue. To know that you can speak good into existence is great, but our words hold enough weight to speak death as well. Death can be negativity. Death can be gossiping about a rumor that went around at your job that may or may not be true. Death can even be the unencouraging words you spoke to your friend in a jokingly way. The truth is that we all have experienced death through the words that someone has spoken to us. And if you haven't, I will be the first to admit, I have experienced a part of me die all because of the careless words someone spoke to me that were not saturated in grace and love. What I want you to see here is that if you know that the words you speak can be used to bring death upon someone or something, we need to try our best to only speak life into the things and the people around us.

Using your words for good, it's about how you say it

Knowing that our words have power is great, but it's also important to make sure that you're using your words for good and not evil. When knowing the power of your words and believing in what you speak, make sure that you're speaking life and not death. How many times have we found ourselves in a situation where someone we were close to was wrong and we wanted to correct them or maybe someone hurt our feelings and we wanted to express that to them. What I'm saying to you is to be careful of how you speak to others. Proverbs 15:4 (NKJV) tells us, *"A wholesome tongue is a tree of life, but perverseness in it breaks the spirit."*

The Message (MSG) Bible says it like this, *"Kind words heal and help; cutting words wound and maim."* So if you're trying to judge if your words are kind or cutting, ask yourself, "Are the words that I am about to speak going to help and heal this individual, or are they just going to make me feel better about the situation?" Ask yourself, "Are the words that I am about to speak going to leave this individual wounded for a period of time?" My friends, lace your words with love when speaking in any manner because the words you are about to speak have the power to produce. Let's vow to produce life.

How do I speak life?

In the book of Genesis during the time when God was creating the world, on every account, it leads with, "God said…" and then follows with, "And there was…" or "And it was so…" This is a testament to God's faith in Himself, which is the same level of faith that we should have in Him. It is important to note that before God spoke light, there was no light. Before He spoke it, it did not exist. What I'm saying to you, my brothers and my sisters, is that in order to use your words to speak life and positivity, you have to speak it even if you don't see it. You have to speak life over the dead things, speak prosperity of the dying things, and speak into existence the things that are yet still nonexistent. Then have the faith to know that it will come to fruition. Though you may feel down and feel like you are not enough, you have to speak it even if you don't feel it, even if you don't see it. Speak the words, "*I am more than enough.*"

I know how hard it is because I was there. I was in a place where someone who I valued told me I was not good enough. I found myself asking God, "What did I do wrong? How was I not enough? I have lived my entire life sold out for You, abstaining from the things of the world so that You could use me, and here I am being rejected and torn down." All this took place literally minutes before God told me to go on a thirty-one-day spiritual fast, not knowing that this commitment was going to cost me people I thought I needed.

When I was still sulking in the pain, God spoke to me and said, "Stay focus. You still have an agenda to fulfill." I began to cry out to God for answers and understanding, and then the same scripture began repeating in my head, "*I am fearfully and wonderfully made. I am fearfully and wonderfully made.*" And then, it hit me. The scripture that I was repeating is how my God felt about me and the words that were spoken to me by man did not resemble what God had said about me in the least bit. Immediately, I began to realize the trick of the enemy.

> *For we wrestle not against flesh and blood, but against principalities, against powers, against the rulers of the darkness of this world, against spiritual wickedness in high places.* (Ephesians 6:12)

My fight was not with the individual; it was with the one who was using them to attack me. When Satan attacks, he starts with your mind and your thoughts because what you think, eventually your body will follow.

Growing up, I attended middle school in Detroit, every morning we, as a school, would recite our school pledge. One student would stand and say, "Why should you watch your thoughts?" Everyone else would respond and say, "Because they become our words." The student would then ask, "Why should you watch your words?" and we'd respond and say, "Because they become our actions."

As a kid, thirteen years old and full of childish thoughts and intentions, you could not have told me that this pledge, that I dreaded to recite so much because I thought it was silly, would make it into the book I would write in the future. But the truth is, our words hold so much weight more than we even know.

Once I realized what the enemy was doing, trust me, it did not get better immediately afterward. But I told myself that I would not allow the enemy to win, and so I spoke against every lie that was spoken to me. And with tears in my eyes and pain in my heart, I fell to my knees and began to cry out to God, and I began to speak the words, "I am more than enough." And because I spoke those words over my life and because I began to believe them (even though I didn't feel like it in the moment and it went against what I had just been told). You are reading this book today, hopefully being encouraged and your faith is being renewed and restored.

CHAPTER 2

Speak Up!

We learned in the previous chapter that there is power in our words. Now it's time to use them and speak up. It's not enough just to know if you don't use what you know. Activate what you know. Too often, we sit down on the knowledge that could help someone else or even ourselves because we are afraid to speak. I have even been guilty of it.

Anyone who knows me will tell you how quiet I was as a child, hesitant to speak up and very shy. Years later, in my adulthood, God called me to be a teacher where you literally have to talk all day and every day and often repeat yourself multiple times all while trying to practice having patience. What I'm saying is that when God has a call on your life, often it will make you feel uncomfortable. God does not work in comfort zones. If we are going to accept the call to be more than enough, we can't be afraid to allow God to expand us so that we can break the boundaries and the walls of our comfort zone. It's time out for mediocracy, and it's time to speak up.

Speak up about what you want

As believers, what we want should align with God's Word and what God wants for us as well. John 10:10 (NKJV) says, *"I have come that they may have life and that they might have it more abundantly.*" God wants you to have life and to have more than enough to sustain it. The Message Bible says it like this, "*I came so they can have real and eternal life, a more and better life than they ever dreamed of.*" The truth is that God wants more for us than we want for ourselves. The Word says, "A better life than they ever dreamed of." God's intentions and dreams for us are bigger than our own.

I want you to think of where you see yourself in ten years, think about all the things you want to acquire in the future. Now imagine all of that times ten. That's what God is saying when He says "more abundantly." *Abundant* means available in large quantities, plentiful, or having plenty of. Abundance is overflow. God wants for you to have and to be more than enough. So the question to ask yourself is, "Do you really want what God wants for you?"

What I have come to find out is that not all the time, what we want aligns with what God wants for us and not all the time, what God wants for us aligns with what we want for ourselves. The truth of the matter is that there is a heavy weight on us in saying we want whatever God wants for us. This statement embodies a higher level of surrendering because what you are really saying is, "God, I give my desires over to You. Do in me and with me whatever You want to do." When we really look at this statement, one has to have reached a point in their life where they have tried fulfilling their own destiny and their own desires and it just hasn't worked out and now they are saying, "God do You in *me*." We as people don't want to hear that, in order to live in Christ, we have to die to ourselves (Galatians 2:20). Meaning, that our wants are going to have to change to match what God wants for us; it's an act of sacrifice.

Speak up about who you believe

It's time-out for being shy and timid about what we believe in. It's time to speak out about it. If you believe in God, tell someone. Matthew 10:33 says, *"But whoever denies me before men, him I will also deny before my father who is in heaven."* The Message (MSG) Bible says, *"Stand up for me against world opinion and I'll stand up for you before my Father in heaven. If you turn tail and run, do you think I'll cover for you?"* I don't know about you, my friend, but I want Jesus to own me and cover for me. I want Him to recognize me as His own, but we have to proclaim Him to be ours as well.

Too often, we want to settle for a closed door, one-sided relationship with Christ. We pray to Him to do something great in our lives, He does it, and then we never tell anyone. There aren't too many of us who will remain in a relationship with someone who never tell others that they are in a relationship with us. But somehow, we think God is okay with it. The problem is that too many of us want God to show up on our behalf, but we want Him to do it behind closed doors. I want to awaken something inside of you and tell you to stop sitting on what God is doing and what He has done for you. That very thing is your testimony, and you have to speak up and talk about it.

I want to enlighten someone really quick and tell you that if you are struggling with using your words to testify on what God has done in your life, it's because you haven't acknowledged what God has done for you as being something that God has done for you. What are you saying, April? What I am saying to you is that maybe you can't speak about your testimonies because you haven't identified them as being testimonies. I want to free you and tell you that your past and who you used to be is not something that you put on the back burner and forget about because you don't want to revisit it. It's not for you to revisit; it's for you to recite. That very thing is your testimony—so speak it! If it hurt you, it's your testimony. If it broke you, it's your testimony. If it changed you or helped you, it's your testimony. Don't leave God showing up in your life in the closet... Speak up and tell the world that "I serve a God, and I know He's real because he's done XYZ for me." And be bold about it, my friend.

I want to help someone get delivered who may be struggling with speaking on your past and using it as a testimony, you're probably saying, "I don't want to tell people about my past because then I have to revisit it and it's just too painful still, and I don't want people to know about that part of me." I want to help you by telling you that what you're experiencing is not the absence of a testimony or your inability to speak up but rather your soul not having accepted the deliverance that God wants to give you from your past. Someone else is depending on your deliverance so that you can speak your testimony. It's your specific testimony that can help someone else going through the same thing that you were already brought out of. So I urge you, my brothers and my sisters, to speak up.

If we are going to speak up about who we believe in, we don't only need to be vocal about what He's done for us, but we also need to be bold about who He is to us. I'm not just talking about in your daily life. Yes, it is important to not be ashamed to be on God's side, but also, let's not be ashamed when it comes to offering up a sacrifice of praise. It's easy to praise God for bringing you through something, but what about while you're still in the storm? What about when you can't remember the last financial blessing or the last time your body was healed? Can you still find the gratitude to praise God simply for who He is?

Too often, we leave praise and worship to those who have a massive testimony, but let me stop you there because we all have something that God has done for us. But let's not put God in a box because this book is about breaking down boundaries and walls. Let's not just praise when life is good. Praise when life is bad. Praise when you feel alone and forgotten. Praise God because He is deserving of our praise just because of who He is. It's time-out for us being silent about God during praise and worship. You've mastered the art of letting your words speak on Him. Now it's time to let your praise speak of Him.

Speak up about what you believe—your values

As believers, one thing that is absolutely essential in our walk with Christ is values. In fact, it is our values that set us apart from the world. It is our values that make us not like everybody else. If we are going to be bold in this life in Christ, let's go all the way. The world needs to see true believers who have made the vow to follow through with what the Word says.

What I have learned (and this is just my personal story) is that it's really hard to speak up about values. I had no problem living out my values in Christ, but sharing them was where I struggled, and I don't think I'm the only one, especially when we live in a world that normalizes all the things that God tells us not to do. I found myself not being so open to talk about the act of abstaining from premarital sex, alcohol, the use of drugs, and even profanity because it has become so taboo. But I want to help anyone who may be feeling like me or you're struggling to decide if you should abstain from certain things because of how the world views it or because of how you may be viewed in the world. I want you to know that you are not of the world. We are in the world to let our light (the light of Christ) shine. Your life is going to be someone's conviction and testimony.

John 17:16–19 (MSG) says,

> *They are no more defined by the world than I am defined by the world. Make them holy—consecrated—with the truth; your word is consecrating truth. In the same way you gave me a mission in the world, I give them a mission in the world. I'm conse-*

crating myself for their sakes, so they'll be truth-consecrated in their mission.

The KJV replaces the word *consecrate* with the word *sanctify*. *Sanctify* simply means to set apart or declare holy for God's use. Jesus is telling us that we are not to be like the world even though we are in the world. Our talk should be different, our walk should be different, and how we act should be different. And then He tells us that we will be sanctified through His truth which is the Word. Meaning, that the Word is all the validation and truth we need for as to why we live the way we live, and we should be able to stand bold and firm on His Word knowing that it is true.

So if you find yourself struggling to stand bold in your Christ lifestyle, remember that you should not judge or base your lifestyle on what the world is doing because we are not of the world; and therefore, the only validation that we need is the truth that is revealed through God's Word.

Speak up about what you believe—your visions

This is probably one of my favorites because visions are so personal, but that doesn't mean you have to be silent about them. Often when God gives us visions for a business plan or something of big magnitude, others that don't have the same vision will criticize and critique what God has told you, and that's okay. Keep believing in God to do big things in your life. Don't be timid about the things that God has revealed to you. If God gave you the vision, He is faithful to perform it. If people don't look at your visions and say you're crazy or that it won't work, then you are not dreaming big enough.

I want you to reach down inside for the dreams and the visions that only God can fulfill. As believers, we can no longer sale ourselves, or the God we serve, short. So dream bigger than others can imagine. Activate your faith and give God time to show up on your behalf in the presence of your doubters. More than enough is what our dreams should be. Our visions should be extra, excessive, and out of this world. I believe that some of us, including myself, are sitting on million-dollar visions because we are afraid of what people may say and it seems nearly impossible. In 2 Timothy 1:7, it tells us that "God has not given us the spirit of fear but of power and of love and of a sound mind."

Don't let fear intimidate you from living out loud and fulfilling your dreams. Speak up and be bold about what God has planted inside of you, and do not shrink for anyone.

Often, I think we allow our vision to intimidate us because we tell small-minded people what God has told us, and all they end up doing is deterring us from our calling. Matthew 7:6 tells us not to cast our pearls before swine. Not everyone is worthy of hearing what God has told you. Some just have to sit and watch from afar. Don't let their inability to see what God showed you obstruct your view. The vision is still good.

Visions are not only personal, but they also are a test of faith. God never gives visions that can be done overnight. But rather, He'll give you a vision that will test your faith and will take time to perfect. Your faith and dedication will determine the unveiling of your vision. Whether or not you believe it will happen, and actually, put forth the effort to make it happen, will determine whether or not it will actually happen. When God gives you a vision, be bold about it and have confidence. Have confidence in the vision but also in the God who provided the visions.

CHAPTER 3

Have Faith

Though our values play a huge role in our walk with Christ, there would be no values or even a walk with Christ if we didn't have faith. Faith is the essence of our walk with Christ. Without faith, we can't really call ourselves true Christians. Believe it or not, people (the world) are looking to see just how real and useful your faith is, just to see if it's worth them trying.

As believers, we should be the examples to the world. If the world sees you holding on to your faith and things actually begin to turn around for your good, they will then begin to acquire curiosity about the God we serve. And that's how we win souls. The thing about faith is that it's more than just believing in God, but rather, it is the act of believing God. To believe in God is great. Our salvation is the evidence that shows we believe in God. But it's our faith that says we believe God.

I have come to find out that there are too many Christians that believe in God but lack the faith to believe God. Great, you know God exists. But do you know what His Word says, and do you really believe it? A lot of us would answer so quickly and say, "Yes, I know what the Word says, and I believe it."

Romans 8:28 tells us that all things work together for our good. If I asked you if you really believed that scripture, you would probably say yes. But what about when you are in the midst of the worst storm of your life. You have lost your job, your friends are few, you've discovered a new sickness in your body, and nothing seems to be making sense. Could you still reach down inside and find Romans 8:28 and believe it? The truth is most of us would ask God, "Why me?" before we even begin to activate our faith in God's Word.

It was in the book of Job where Job experienced trauma after trauma. Even though he was given double, in the end, there was still a point where Job spoke and said, "May the day perish on which I was born" in Job 3:3. Job became weary in his trails just like we as Christians do now. It was in Job 13:15 where Job has a response and says, "*Though he slay me, yet will I trust him.*" I want for us to get to a point where we have a Job 13:15 response through the entire storm. No matter how bad it may look or how bad it may get, we can continue to trust and thank God.

It's clear to me that even though faith is a very crucial part of being a Christian, one of the hardest things for us as Christians to do is actually have faith.

What is faith?

First things first, we won't ever be able to obtain something if we don't know what it really is. So what exactly is faith? I want to pause here because too many of us confuse faith with the act of salvation. We equate being a Christian to having faith, when in reality, as a Christian, we should have faith, but it doesn't always work that way, and I am not here to condemn any Christian who may be discovering that your faith is not where it should be. Too often, we portray being Christian as an immediate change in behavior, but truth be told, this is a process, and acquiring strong faith is also a process. But maybe, so many of us lack faith because we don't really know what it is.

Hebrews 11:1 (KJV) tells us that faith is the substance of things hoped for, the evidence of things not seen. The Message Bible says that it's our handle on what we can't see. But what does this phrase, "The substance of things hoped for" really mean? I was an English major in college, and I believe that this is what you would call an oxymoron. The Bible is telling us that faith is a substance and hope all at the same time. A *substance* is something that can be touched, and *hope* is something that you can't see or touch, so how can faith—also something you can't touch—be substance and hope all at the same time?

Hebrews 11:1 also says that it is the evidence of things not seen. How can there be evidence for something that we can't see (faith) of the things not seen? If you're reading this and haven't yet figured out what an oxymoron is, it's the contradictory of words in the English language. It's the opposites. So what is faith? *Faith* is the contradiction of what you see. It's the opposite of what you see, the opposite of your situation. Your situation says you're sick; faith says you're already healed. Your situation says there's no way out; faith says God has already made a way. Life says no; faith steps in and says yes. Faith contradicts what we can see. So I encourage you to look at your life now and to think on the areas of your life that may seem impossible to solve, and I want you to begin to speak the opposite of what you see. That, my friend, is faith.

Why do we struggle with having faith?

We know what faith is, but we still struggle to have it. I want to suggest that maybe we still struggle to have faith because we as humans that are of the flesh struggle to believe what we can't see. I just told you that faith is the opposite of what you see. But it still isn't enough just to know; we have to activate it. Having faith is not an easy task; it's nearly crazy. Matter of fact, if people don't think you are crazy for the kind of faith that you have, then you are not doing it right. You know you have faith when you believe God for things that others don't. The truth behind faith is that it's a measure of your maturity in God. You can see how mature someone is in Christ based on the kind of faith they have. Your level of faith exposes your maturity in Christ, and so the question is, "Can your faith move a mountain?" (Mark 11:22–23).

Faith forces us to believe before we can see it. What that means is that you have to see it (in the spirit) before you see it (in the physical). I challenge you, my brothers and my sisters. You may have questionable faith that isn't where you think it should be. I urge you to ask God to develop your faith and your maturity as well. Because with great faith comes an even greater level of maturity. James 4:2 says you have not because you ask not. You have acknowledged that your faith could be greater. Now put it into action and ask God for what you lack.

Keep your faith

Once you have discovered faith and have obtained the faith that can move a mountain, hold on to it. Once you get a hold on faith, get a real good grip and don't let go because life is going to happen and your faith will be tested. Use the test as moments to grow your faith even deeper. Hebrews 11:6 tells us that "without faith, it is impossible to please God." God is pleased with your faith, not just because you have it or because you are so impressive but because you have activated a higher level of trust in Him, that at the end of the day, glorifies God.

Too often, we allow unforeseen circumstances to cause our faith to waver. I want us to get to a place where we are unstoppable and we can say that no matter what comes our way, we will not lose our faith in God because your faith confuses the enemy. Satan will not know what to do when you begin to praise God in your pain. And let us be honest, sometimes we need to confuse ourselves. Sometimes you have to "faith" your way through your hurt because sulking in your pain is not going to bring you out of it. It's time to live out loud, activate your Job 13:15 attitude, and "faith" your way through it.

We have to get to a point where we become fighters. Truth be told, we are at war with everything that comes our way that does not reflect God's Word. If I'm being completely honest with you, in order to keep your faith, you are going to have to fight for it. It will not be easy to speak the opposite of what we see. We are in a daily fight to kill our reality. We can't truly and fully activate our Job 13:15 faith if we don't learn to activate our inner man or our spirit man first. Our flesh will never have the capacity nor the capability to even fathom the faith that we need to have in order to boldly walk in Christ. Knowing this, it is our duty to grow our spirit man so that we can begin to fully live and walk in the faith that pleases God.

Put your faith to work

Now that you know what faith is and how we should use it, it's now time to use it. We have to put our faith to work. James 2:17 tells us that faith without works is dead. Yes, speaking what you want and what you believe is very crucial when it comes to having faith. But what good is it to have faith that God will get you a job and then you never fill out any job applications? We have to meet God halfway.

Too often, we want God to do all the work through "faith." What God really wants is for us to work our faith. If you believe God can get you the house, then make the first steps to apply. God wants to know how much you really have faith in Him. The kind of faith that will take the first steps even when you can't see the next steps.

CHAPTER 4

Stand Out

As children of God, it's important that we become mindful that we don't just talk about the Word but that we are also doers of the Word (James 1:22). Don't just talk about it; be about it. We are quick to quote what the Word says in some instances while simultaneously neglecting to embody what it says on other occasions. God wants consistency and dedication.

Too often, we pick and choose what we want to follow in God's Word. Deciding to only go so far for God (when it comes to how we live our lives) is similar to us being on the fence. In Revelations 3:16, Jesus says, *"So then because thou art lukewarm, and neither cold nor hot, I will spue thee out of my mouth."* God is saying that you being on the fence about your walk with Him (meaning, you are not all in neither are you all out) bothers Him more than the nonbeliever.

The Word says He spits out the lukewarm individual. God wants for all of us to decide whose side we are going to be on. To reject the things of God is to accept the things of the world. In 2 Corinthians 4:4 (NLT), it tells us that Satan is the god of the world. So by choosing to indulge in the things of the world is just as saying, "I would much rather take what Satan has to offer than what God has to offer." That is a dangerous decision to make, especially if you lack the knowledge to know what exactly it is that you are agreeing to.

Second Corinthians 4:4 (NLT) also says that the god of the world has blinded the minds of those who don't believe. They are unable to see the glorious light of the good news. When we agree to blend in with the world, we are saying that the god of the world (Satan) is who we are serving at that given moment. He then has the ability to blind those individuals from the truth about Christ. And this is why God despises lukewarm behavior.

When you partake in the worldly behaviors, you are under the influence of Satan. When you partake in godly behaviors, you are under the influence of the Holy Spirit. When you do both, you are doing what is called serving two gods. Mathew 6:24 says that no one can serve two masters for either he will hate one and love the other or be loyal to one and despise the other. God doesn't want the "on the fence Christian" because one day, you will love Him and the next day you will not. While you're at church, you love God. But when you're out with your friends partaking in behaviors that don't bring Him glory, you love Satan.

Just about all of us would say that we love God without any hesitation, but the Word is telling us that when we serve two masters, it's impossible to love both. If you love God, show it. Love is an action word, and if we proclaim to love God, we need to keep His commandments (John 14:15).

Live it

I want to be as honest and transparent as possible here. If we are going to be true believers and live out loud, we have to take charge and live out the Word of God. When you make the decision to live out God's Word, you are also taking the stand to be different. The problem with most people, especially from my generation, is that we have a fear of being different and not fitting in. Everyone wants to be down, and everyone wants to be cool.

If I'm going to be transparent, I have to admit that I have never really been able to "fit in." My whole life, I have been *different*. Before I ever really chose to live for God completely, I still struggled to fit in. Initially, it was a matter of me not fitting the physical criteria to fit in with certain groups. As I began to grow in God, it became others not meeting my standards of who I wanted to surround myself with. I became uncomfortable around certain people because their actions were not a reflection of God. I will admit that even after me deciding to live for God, I still struggled with fitting in and making friends. I found myself being laughed at and judged because of how I was. I couldn't understand the criticism at the moment, but Matthew 5:11 tells us that you are blessed when they revile and persecute you and say all kinds of evil against you falsely for God's sake. People's rejection and criticism about how you live your life in Christ is a reflection of them. What they are really saying is that your life is convicting them and beginning to make them feel uncomfortable. But *continue to live the truth* which is the Word of God.

If I am being completely honest, there are moments during my walk with Christ now when I still question my isolation from people. I have always felt "reserved." I wondered why I couldn't fit into certain crowds and still love Jesus. It was to the point where my "church" friends were even few. And I was beginning to ask God what is it about me that I can't have friends. God spoke to me one night and told me so clearly that my states of isolation are much bigger than me but that He has me in a season of solitude so that He can pour into me without risking the chance of His anointing being wasted or drained because I'm connected to the wrong people.

His Spirit spoke to me and said, "April, what I have placed inside of you is too important to be in the presence of people who can't go where I'm taking you. I need you to birth something, and certain people are only going to help you abort the gift and not birth it."

I want to reach out to someone who may be feeling like me, living in constant stages of isolation with little to no friends or companionships. I want to tell you that you are not in this season by happenstance, but God has something He needs you to do. So utilize your solitude to grow in God.

I feel that we, especially my younger audience, often thwart what God is trying to do in us and with us because we relate our singleness and us being alone as something bad. Instead of getting in the presence of God, we stress about not having the presence of man. Allow your solitude to grow you so that you can fully live for God without any regrets.

If we are going to live out God's Word, we have to come to an understanding that there are certain things we can't do. This is the part that is hard for most people because all the things that we are banned from as believers are all governed by self. So in order to abstain from the things that are not of God, you have to die to your self. We have to get to a place where we are living in the spirit and so our spirit can override our flesh in ungodly behaviors.

Everything about us should be different as followers of Christ. We should resemble Christ. How we talk should be different, such as profanity, criticism, and even gossiping. We read earlier that there is power in our words, and we visited Proverbs 15:4 that tells us a wholesome tongue is a tree of life. Your words should only produce positivity and life. Not only should our talk be different but how we walk and how we live our lives should be different. We cannot indulge in the things of world because in doing so, you are under the influence of another master, and the Word already tells us that it is not possible to serve two masters in Matthew 6:24.

As men and women of God, we should be sanctified—set apart for God's use. We need to be aware of where we are, who we are with, and what we are doing because God is looking to use us at any moment and we need to be available to answer the call, or else, He will find someone else to bring His name glory.

I don't know about you, but I have a spirit that says, "When everyone else is reluctant or can't be found, I'll be the one, God, that You can use to bring Your name glory."

Sanctification says that God sets us apart for His use. What that means is that if you are not set apart from the world, God can't reach you while you are entertaining crowds of people that aren't bringing you closer to God. This doesn't mean that God can't use people who used to have a past. However, God wants to use you in your sanctified form, when you resemble Him and not the god of the world. So often, God will clean you up so that He can use you.

Be about God's business

If we are going to stand out, we don't only need to live like Christ, but we also need to be about God's business. What exactly is God's business? God's business is to save souls. The whole point of God sending His son, Jesus Christ, to be crucified was for the souls of man. To give us a chance to be redeemed and saved through the crucifixion of Jesus Christ. To be crucified is to be lifted up. In order for Jesus to die on the cross, the cross had to be lifted up. In John 12:32, Jesus said, "If I be lifted up, I will draw all people to Myself." It is the crucifixion of Christ that is our gateway into heaven. So how do we as believers be about God's business? Well, we lift Him up. It's as simple as that. We lift up His name.

There are multiple ways that we can lift up our Father in heaven. One way is with our life. You can lift up God just by how you live. What God really wants is for us to glorify Him. Your life alone should glorify God. We should have a natural desire as believers to glorify Christ with our lives. Take some time to evaluate your life and your daily routine, and ask yourself if what you are doing is glorifying God. Ask yourself, "If God came into my situation right now, would He be pleased? If the cover was pulled off from me right now and my life was on display to the whole world, would it draw people closer to God?"

Too often, we live our lives thinking that because man can't see us, it's okay, but what about what God can see? Everything we do, no matter where we are, should bring God glory.

We shouldn't only glorify God with our lives but also through praise and worship because those are our intimate moments with God. It is during praise and worship that we allow the Holy Spirit to come in and do supernatural things in our presence. For most people, especially lost souls, convincing comes through personal experiences and physical encounters. They need to see God at work through you. They need to see and feel the presence of the Holy Spirit and the power of prayer. If someone of the world comes in contact with you and you claim to be a believer but refuse to have spiritual praise and worship encounters with the God you claim to be so good, do you really think they are going to be drawn to the God you serve? You won't even praise Him, so why should they?

The Bible says that if Christ be lifted up, then He'll draw men unto Him. We have to get to a point where we get out of ourselves and realize that this is bigger than us. It's about God, and if we're going to be about God's business, we want to lift Him up so high that people begin to wonder who is this good God that we're speaking of.

As much as our job is to lift up the name of Jesus with our lives and with our praise and worship, we also need to be in position to lift Him up with our words. As believers, every chance we get, we should be finding ways to give God the glory. That doesn't mean we have to force God on everyone we come in contact with, but a simple, "I just got a brand-new car. God is so good" will suffice. God wants us to not be ashamed and to give honor where honor is due.

We are also called to evangelize to people. That simply means to tell people about God when opportunity shows itself. We need to be about God's business, the business that is into saving souls, because it's bigger than us. If we are going to be more than enough and live out loud, we have to come out of ourselves and let God have His way.

Have a relationship with God

Lastly, if we are going to stand out, we absolutely have to have relationship with God. In fact, without a relationship with God, none of what has been mentioned in this chapter will be obtainable. So if you've been reading this chapter and have struggled to process what God is calling you to do for Him, it may be because you lack relationship or a strong relationship with Christ.

In the Bible, we are referred to as the bride of Christ in Ephesians 5:22, where the Word compares the physical marriage to that of the relationship between the church and Christ. Too often, we hear people talk about having a relationship with Christ, but we rarely ever hear people talk about what exactly makes a good relationship with Christ. I want to help you develop and grow your relationship with Christ by telling you that there are three things that we need to have a good relationship with God. Just like any healthy marriage, we need communication, submission, and intimacy.

Two things to know about having good communication. One, it needs to be direct; and two, it needs to be consistent. How do we communicate with God? Through prayer. First, our communication needs to be clear and direct. Who are you talking to? Matthew 6:9 tells us that when we pray, we need to acknowledge who we are talking to. Address the Father. Hebrews 4:16 (KJV) says, "*Let us come boldly to the throne of grace.*" The Message Bible says, "*Let's walk right up to him and get what he is ready to give.*" So be direct and bold when talking to God.

When you are trying to communicate with your boss or someone in authority, you don't just start talking at them while neglecting eye contact and without addressing them by name; therefore, we should do our God the same way. We need to approach Him with reverence and also with faith.

Our communication should not just be direct, but it also should be consistent (1 Thessalonians 5:17). We need to be in constant prayer with God. If we want our relationships in Christ to flourish, we need to pray on the regular.

Too often, we only turn to God when we feel like it or when life is rough or when we need something. But our prayer life needs to be growing daily. Our prayers to God should go beyond what we want, but we need to also become intercessors for others. When your prayer life is growing, you'll find yourself going to God for others more than yourself. Philippians 4:6 (MSG) says, *"Don't fret or worry. Instead of worrying, pray. Let petitions and praises shape your worries into prayers."* Pray constantly but not just for you but also for others as well.

Not only do we need a consistent and direct prayer life in our relationship with God, we also need submission. Every good marriage has a healthy balance of submission. Our marriage with Christ should have the same healthy balance of submission. Our relationship with God should consist of us submitting to the Holy Spirit. I want to say, if you don't have submission to the Holy Spirit, you will never be able to truly be intimate with God; it's impossible. Our submission to the Holy Spirit is us letting go of our self and giving God permission to use us supernaturally, not just physically.

Too often, we say that we are Christians, but we secretly are afraid of the Holy Spirit. And we have portrayed the Holy Spirit as being something freaky that you can catch. I want to change your thinking because in order to be able to submit to the Holy Spirit, you have to realize that the Holy Spirit is a someone and not a something. He's a person—a who, not an it. And He is an experience, not something you can catch. Until you get that in your spirit, you will never be able to submit to Him until you change your view of Him.

So if you want your relationship to grow in God but you lack submission to the Holy Spirit, ask the Holy Spirit to reveal Himself to you because, believe it or not, He longs for you to know Him better, but He will not beg you. He wants you to choose Him. Truth is, you cannot be everything God has called you to be without the Holy Spirit. It's the Holy Spirit that gives us power.

Some of us are wondering why we lack power to do supernatural things, and we even lack the power to get prayers through. I believe that there are too many scripture quoting Christians and not enough power holding Christians. Acts 1:8 says, *"You shall receive power when the Holy Spirit has come upon you."* Your lack of power is the absence of the Holy Spirit. So I challenge all of you to really seek the face of God and acquire and desire to receive an experience with the Holy Spirit.

Lastly, to have a healthy relationship with God, you need intimacy. Intimacy with God is when we take time to reverence and acknowledge God through praise and worship. Praise and worship is how we as Christians incorporate intimacy into our relationship with God. One can't truly have a good marital connection without intimacy. How can we call ourselves the bride of Christ without intimacy? We absolutely must praise God. It is not an option.

I could go through the entire book of Psalms and quote so many scriptures on praise and worship, but I won't because you'd be reading all day. But that's how important praise is to God. I could write an entire book on praise and worship alone. However, I will give you this scripture instead. Psalm 150:6 (MSG) says, *"Let every living, breathing creature praise God!"* We must praise God; that's how we build intimacy.

We already know that the Word tells us that when we lift up Christ, souls will be saved (John 12:32). Someone's salvation is depending on your praise. How can you claim to be about God's business, which is saving souls, if you don't do the one thing that brings in souls? *Lift Him up!*

I have come to realize that there are too many Christians who know the Word, have a desire to live for God, and still lack the relationship. For some, it may be the fear of submitting and having to give up control of your own life, and for others, maybe it's the fear of not being able to fully live for God. I want to say to both of those individuals that what you are feeling is completely normal. Every good and real Christian has had an "I didn't feel worthy enough" in them at some point during their salvation. But I want to comfort you in letting you know that you don't have to take these steps toward a higher calling in Christ on your own. Jesus will be with you every step of the way.

Truth be told, there is no way anyone can live this life for Christ without the help of Christ. But the good news is He never told us that we had to do it by ourselves. Your spirit is saying that you can't live for Christ because you're too far gone and you're life is too messy. But God is still saying, "Come and let Me do the change in you. I don't want you to do it by yourself because you won't be able to without My power. Let Me give you the power of My Holy Spirit through relationship. I will help you live for Me."

Personally, I love God because He doesn't leave us to live for Him by ourselves. He left His Holy Spirit to help and guide us, and that is good news (John 14:16–17).

CHAPTER 5

See It

Jesus wants us to live and to have an abundant life (John 10:10). His Word says that He came so that we would have life and have it more abundantly, but the question is, can we see that for ourselves? If we are going to live out loud and receive the life that is more than enough, we must change the way we think. Most importantly, we must change the way we think of ourselves. We will never be able to have more than enough nor will we be able to be more than enough if we don't see it for ourselves.

The problem with most people struggling to see themselves living in an abundant life, is the fact that they don't see themselves worthy of a lifestyle that steps outside of the mediocracy that they have become so accustom to living in. Too often, we as believers become satisfied with having just enough instead of more than enough.

It's a mindset

"More than enough" is not just a saying we say to make us feel good about ourselves, and though it is a lifestyle, it's a lifestyle that starts within our mind. Your thinking has to change, which will ultimately change the way you view yourself. God told us in Psalm

139:14 that we are fearfully and wonderfully made. He told us that we were created in His image (Genesis 1:27). Therefore, God sees each of us as worthy to receive His blessings and abundance. At the end of the day, He saw us worthy of sending His only son to die for our sins, knowing that so many people still would not choose Him (John 3:16).

The sad truth is that, if most of us were asked who we were or to describe ourselves, most of us would make note of all the things that people say about us or all the things that people know us by. Unfortunately, nine times out of ten, none of us, if asked to describe ourselves, would use the words more than enough, worthy, or of great value. Instead, we would say things like outgoing or reserved, self-motivated or compassionate.

God wants us to adapt the same thoughts that He has toward us in terms of worth. When Jesus died on the cross, He died for our sins while we were yet still sinners (Romans 5:8). And not only that, He also took on all of our sins even though He lived a sinless life. When we really look at the kind of love that God has for us, what the Word is really saying is that God loved us while we were sinners, in all of our mess, and even when we felt unworthy. God looked at us and saw the worth under the wretch. So if we were created in His image and we are to strive to be like Christ, why can't we see ourselves to be of the same worth that God saw in us?

I want to argue that this is so because we have not taken the time to adapt a new mindset toward ourselves. The enemy wants you to look at all your faults, shortcomings, and mistakes and to rob yourself of the opportunity to allow God's love to overshadow your wrongs. The enemy doesn't want you to see or know your worth. Once we begin to see our worth, we then begin to act accordingly.

Do better

The enemy doesn't want you to think for one second that you deserve better because in knowing better, you begin to do better. When we take time to evaluate the things in our life that we are tolerating but as a child of God, we should not be putting up with, we then begin to make decisions that better represent our worth. And if that means walking away from people, places, and bad habits that keep us in bondage, then so be it.

The truth behind your worth is that the enemy knows exactly what God has placed inside of you. He sees your anointing before you even know you're anointed. With that being said, he will try everything in his power to deter and hinder you from reaching your goal in Christ. The easiest way for Satan to attack is through your thoughts. If he can convince you to think less of yourself, he can keep you trapped in a place, doing things that do not represent the God we serve. So ask yourself, "Am I settling for this lifestyle because this is what I feel I deserve? Does this lifestyle accurately represent the life that Christ has called me to live?"

Too many of us end up in cycles because we haven't established our worth. We know right from wrong. We know what the Word says, but it seems as though we just keep falling into the same sins over and over again. We find ourselves in these places because what we allow is a reflection of how we see ourselves. If I took a poll on how many people, in a room full of one hundred people, knew their worth, one hundred hands would go up to proclaim that they all know their worth. If I were to evaluate those same one hundred individuals' lives, just about all of them would be living in a situation that God did not ordain for them and that doesn't attest to their worth in Christ.

What I'm saying is that most of us have worth that comes with limitations. We know our worth in certain circumstances but fail to see that same worth in other situations. For example, maybe we won't tolerate disrespect from a significant other, as far as cheating or even physical abuse, but we will subject ourselves to premarital behaviors that don't truly reflect our worth. Once we as believers really see our worth, we won't settle for mediocracy from anyone or in any area of our lives. We will begin to live our lives with an expectancy.

Don't settle

If we are going to see more than enough for ourselves, then we have to take on the character that does not settle. It's easy to say, "I won't settle," but the idea is what exactly won't you settle for? I want to stick a pin here because truth be told, some of us have expectations that are acceptable to the world but not necessarily acceptable to God. If we are going to be all that God has called us to be, our expectations must match God's view of us. After all, Christ deemed us worthy enough to die for. So as believers, there is no room for settling for mediocracy. We have every right not to settle in our relationships, in our careers, and even in our friendships simply because we are children of God.

Not settling means that we have acknowledged our true worth, which is the worth that God sees in us, and we have adapted His principles to our lives and we refuse to settle for anything less than what God has for us. What this means is that we are going to have to surrender our wants and our will to the will of God. We settle for a lot of things simply because they match *our* expectations and not *God's* expectations of what He sees for us. Many of us get stuck in this place because we never consult God before we make moves. Considering God's Word and direction for our life is so crucial when making decisions that represent our worth in Christ.

Reject less so that you can see more

    We never take the time to ask God, "Is this what You desire for me, or is this what I see for myself?" God desires to give all of us His best, but we tend to settle for what is familiar, and most of the time, it is not God's best for us. We have to get to a place where we reject all things that may feel or seem right to us but aren't right in God's view for us. This means rejecting comfort zones.

    A lot of us have a desire to live right and a desire to choose the right people to surround ourselves with, but we tend to repeat cycles that aren't right for us simply because we have become accustom to familiarity. It's not that we like sin or because we like doing what is wrong, but it's the fact that wrong begins to look right when we become comfortable. Often, settling begins to look like we aren't settling because we have become comfortable with settling. And often, less will make you feel uncomfortable unless you have become comfortable with less. Some of us can't even recognize when we are accepting less than what we deserve because we have been doing it for so long and now it has become a place of comfort for us. We even become so sucked in that we will try to convince ourselves and others that our wrong is right. We must be able to reject less so that we can begin to see more for ourselves.

    The truth about more is that God will use more to grow you. In order to grow, you are going to have to expand and leave your comfort zones. So what this means is more, just like growth, will cause you to be uncomfortable. So many of us reject more and growth for the sake of being comfortable. God can't use you to reach souls or to give His name glory in you being comfortable. So it's either God's will or your will. Unfortunately, many people won't ever be able to get to the place where they see more than enough for themselves because they refuse to reject less.

    Rejecting less will leave you in a place where you feel left out, forgotten, and alone. Trust me, I have been there. I have had to walk away from things and people that were not a reflection of my worth. And if I'm being completely honest, it took me some time to get there. Mainly because at the time, what I was accepting is what I thought I deserved. Once I realized my own worth, not the worth I was waiting on man to see but the worth that was already stamped on me at the day of my salvation, I was able to walk out of less and walk into what God had for me.

Yes, I went through a season of feeling alone, forgotten, and even regret, but God used all of that to get something even greater out of me that would benefit more than just my feelings and my emotions. It would benefit people all over the world who needed what I had. God had to get me to a place of submission first. That's what this is all about. We have to submit to God if we want to be able to reject the things of the world and the things that we want but aren't good for us (James 4:7).

CHAPTER 6

Desire It

Once you are able to see more than enough for yourself, it's now time to make it your desire to be and to have more than enough. You have accomplished the mind change, now let us conquer the heart change. Our desires are going to have to change. Psalm 37:4 says that if we delight ourselves in the Lord, then He will give us the desires of our heart. There are two things that we usually miss when reading this scripture because we so eagerly want to get to the end result without fully understanding how to get the end result. Proverbs 4:7 tells us in all our getting to get understanding, so let's get the understanding of what Psalm 37:4 is really saying to us.

The end result is to have our desires be fulfilled, but there is a prerequisite before our desires can be met. The prerequisite is in the scripture. It tells us to "delight ourselves in the Lord." The Message Bible translates this to "keep company with God." What Psalm 37:4 is really saying to us is that we have to find comfort, happiness, and peace in being with God and with being on His side, above all else. Delight yourself in the Lord—be happy in God and be content with doing the things of God—find peace in living for God.

Too many of us forfeit the end result because we neglect to find delight in the Lord. To delight in the Lord means that in all seasons, we're content because we know we're with God. If we're broke, we're still going to delight ourselves in the Lord. If we just lost our job, we're still going to delight ourselves in the Lord. If we just lost a loved one, we're still going to delight ourselves in the Lord.

We want God's promises to be fulfilled in our lives but fail to fulfill our end of the deal. Most of us will only delight ourselves in the Lord during our good seasons, and we begin to feel forsaken in our bad seasons even though God tells us that He will never leave us nor forsake us in Deuteronomy 31:6. If we want the promise of our desires fulfilled, we must first delight ourselves in the Lord no matter where we may be in life.

Secondly, Psalm 37:4 tells us to delight in the Lord and then He will give us the desires of our heart. So many of us get so excited because we think, "Yes, if I just get close to God and if I'm happy with God, then He'll finally give me the man I want or the woman I want or my dream car." But the Word says He will give you the desires of your heart. So many of us take this to mean that everything we desire, He's going to give to us. What this really means is that God is going to give your heart what it should desire.

Here's the revelation. Once you delight yourself in God, once you spend time in His Word and in His presence, there is a heart change that takes place. You will begin to notice the things you used to crave before Christ have become repulsive to you because God is now telling your heart what it should desire. The reality is that so many of us are afraid to delight ourselves in God because we don't want God's desires for us, but rather, we want what we want for us. Well, if God gives us our heart's desires, then who is the author of our wants? The answer is simple; it's not God, but it's actually us. So if we are supposed to be followers of Christ, wanting to see His work done in us, why do we still chase after the things that are obviously not God's plan for us? Maybe for most of us, we have become conflicted with our wants and God's desires.

God's desire versus our wants

We all should desire to live in God's desires for us, but sometimes, it's hard to see that what we think is a God given desire is actually a self-want. So how do we differentiate between the two? If we take the time to look at our wants, they usually lead to a dead end and only benefit one person and that's our self.

Psalm 23:1 says, *"The Lord is my shepherd, I shall not want."* This scripture is telling us that because we look to God for all of our resources, we want nothing because all of our needs are already met. Therefore, when we give in to our wants even though the Bible tells us that all of our needs, God will supply (Philippians 4:19), we are now taking on a spirit of greed. So now we find ourselves having to reject the spirit of greed, covetousness, selfishness, and any other spirit that debunks the thinking that says, "I already have what I need and more." I have learned to work under a belief system that has helped me remain in God's will and not my own.

The belief is simply that God doesn't work with wants but rather needs and desires only. Why do I say this? Well, I believe that God doesn't work with wants because as mentioned, wants can be self-benefitting only, and God wants to do big things in our lives that reach more than just one person. Not only are wants self-benefiting, but they also can be self-led and governed. God wants us to get to a place where we are no longer slaves to our own wills and our own wants, but rather, we are servants to the will of God.

The truth about wants is that they are usually derived from what we see and what we think we need. Sometimes, wants can have so much control over us that they begin to feel like a God given desire. But the Bible tells us that God will give us our desires and that they come from the heart. Wants will always be purposeless; meaning, the very reason for you wanting whatever it is that you want will go no further than your own satisfaction and self-approval. Your wants will have no positive impact on you or anyone else connected to you.

Often when we are living under self-will, it won't even bother us that our wants don't have any positive effect on anyone else because we are making moves for the very purpose of self-fulfillment.

However, desires, in fact, come with a purpose and a purpose that's bigger than just you and me. Anyone can want a new car, but why? Are you going to give the coworker who you know doesn't have a car, a ride to and from work every day? Are you going to make it to your place of worship every Sunday if Jesus blesses you with a new car? It's easy to want to be in a relationship with someone, but when the two of you come together, can you feel and see God's presence in the midst? Or do they just look good to you, do they match your purpose, or do they match your current place? So many of us find ourselves in places where we are trying to force wants to be desires. If you have a true desire to live in God's will, you will become conflicted when you begin to notice that your wants are not bringing God any glory neither do they serve any purpose. Instead, they only glorify yourself. Wants will lead to a dead end, and desires will lead to destiny.

Desires are not conjured up, but rather, they are given. Psalm 37:4 says that God will *give* us the desires of our heart. Desires come directly from God. Some of you may be saying, "My wants feel very much like desires, and sometimes my desires feel very much like wants." This is so because desires are actually wants governed by purpose and ordained by God. The crazy part is that wants and desires will feel exactly the same but lead to a different result. So how do you know which one you're living in before you get to the result? Well, wants will only be beneficial to you. Desires will be beneficial to everything around you. Before you go after something, ask yourself what is your reason for wanting this thing and then ask yourself if it is a God-led mission or a self-led fulfillment. So take a look around and see the state of everything connected to you based off the choices you made. Can you see God's glory in the people, things, and situations you are connected to? And ultimately, can God get the glory out of the people, things, and situations connected to you?

There's one last key identifier of desires. The Bible tells us that God will give you the desires of your *heart*. This is an indicator that desires actually come from the heart, which also signifies that they have to come from a place of love as well. Not love for yourself but a love to produce. Remember, desires lead to purpose, so the very thing your desire should lead you to produce is purpose. Take some time to really sit and evaluate your life and ask yourself, "What in my life has been summoned by a want and not a God-given desire?" and then take time to try and identify if purpose or destiny came with it, or did it only leave you feeling good about obtaining it for a period of time.

Self-will versus God's will

When we as believers take delight in the Lord, it will be obvious because we will acquire a desire to live in God's will and not our own will. And if we find ourselves in a place where we can't quite decipher if we are getting ready to take steps toward our own will or the will of God, we will always consult God before making any moves. Then, get this, the true believer will sit still long enough to hear God's response. So many of us walk into situations that God never gave us permission to access, and we begin to feel as though we have been forsaken by God when things take a turn for the worse simply because we never sat still long enough to actually wait on God's response.

Self-will and flesh will always cause you to hasten the process. On the contrary, God's will, will take you through a process. Don't allow self-will to abort the promise because you wanted to hasten the process. Endure the process; it may get lonely, it may get hard, it may come with betrayal, it may come with disappointment, and it may even come with you having to leave behind everything and everyone you used to know. But the process is worth the promise. God's will is the promise.

God's will is for you to have more than enough, but when you choose your own will over God's will, you trade God's way for your own way. What you're saying is, "God, I don't want what you have to offer. I want what I want because I actually think this is what's best for me." Once you have declared that statement in your heart and with your actions, God steps back.

The Bible says that He stands at the door and He knocks (Revelations 3:20). He will not force His will nor His ways on you, but rather, He gives us free will and the freedom of choice. I love God though because He won't leave us in our bad decisions, but rather, He will continue to keep us in our mess and He's standing with His arms wide open every time we confess our sins and admit our faults, ready to take us in, just as if we never left.

In God's will, there is peace, joy, and purpose. In God's will, there is favor, something that we cannot have outside of His will. His Word says that He gives favor to the righteous (Psalm 5:12). When we step out of God's will, we don't just forfeit purpose and the process, but we also forfeit favor as well. Don't let greed and selfishness cause you to step out of God's will and remove His favor from your life.

Stand still

Allow God's ways to overtake you. So many of us struggle with accepting God's desires for us because we make too many sudden moves. Sometimes, God just wants for us to be still and to stand on His Word (Psalm 46:10). When you find yourself perplexed and cant decipher which way to go, don't continue to make moves in an uncertain direction. Stand still and wait on God. It's in your waiting season when God builds you up.

Isaiah 40:31 tells us that those who wait on the Lord shall renew their strength, mount up with wings, like eagles, and soar. For many of us, we have not been able to soar because we refused to wait. Your waiting seasons build patience, peace, contentment, and then elevation. God tests our patience during our seasons of standing still. He wants to know if you want the promise bad enough to wait for it and to do what He told you to do in this season—whether it's serving, fasting, and praying, or helping others. God wants to know can you activate the spirit of long-suffering (Galatians 5:22)?

After He tests your patience, He'll then put you at peace in your situation. You'll find peace even though you've been praying for it for years and still haven't seen the prayers answered. He'll give you peace even though you see everyone else prospering in the same area you keep failing. The peace that He gives you in this time of waiting will surpass all understanding (Philippians 4:7). Once He gives you the peace to handle the situation, He'll then give you the contentment to remain in the situation without becoming frustrated.

So many of us run from contentment because we think it's the same thing as embracing comfort zones. The difference is that comfort zones are created by us and often causes us to like the situations we're in. Contentment is when we are placed in a situation that may not feel good nor does it match our end result, but it's necessary for the production of our purpose. Therefore, we have to become content with where we have been placed by God.

After contentment comes the elevation. After we have mastered our waiting season, then God will elevate us. That's when we will begin to see our desires fulfilled and an overflow of blessings and opportunity. If you're in a season and you feel like you've been stuck for quite some time now, maybe that's God telling you to be still and wait. After the wait comes strength and elevation. So my question to you is, what are you doing now in your waiting season that is going to get you to the elevation? Are you patient, at peace, and content? If not, then change your posture while you are waiting. God wants to fulfill your desires, and He wants to give you more than enough, but can you wait on it?

CHAPTER 7

Be It

God is calling all of us to be more than enough. You've seen it for yourself. You have made it your desire. Now it's time to actually be it. It's not enough just to talk about it or to know about it if we aren't going to actually be about it.

I want this chapter to help you on a level that goes beyond me just giving you information to enlighten you about your walk with Christ. I want this chapter to shine a light on who you are in Christ, but I also want it to help you see it (more than enough) within yourself.

Self-worth

I feel that the concept of self-worth has been limited to the benefit of women down through the years. However, I want to say that self-worth is for men and women, and it's established through Christ and in His Word. In fact, the acknowledgment of our worth comes from what God has already spoken about us. We begin to develop self-worth when we align our view of ourselves with God's view of us.

If I am going to be completely honest with you, I must admit that I have suffered from the lack of knowledge of my own worth. I lived my life in doubt of who I actually was. Even though I looked like I had it together and though others could see the hand of God on my life, I had let things that I was told and things that I saw and accepted shape my self-worth. I spent very little time actually trying to discover what God had to say about who I was. Instead, I let my own insecurities speak for me. It's hard to say, "I'm more than enough" and to act accordingly when you don't really believe it. Or maybe, you look around at your life and at the decisions you have made and you think to yourself, *Maybe I'm not who I thought I was. Maybe I'm not as great as I have been telling myself.*

I want to argue that it's not a matter of you not being good enough or not being more than enough, but rather, the decisions and the choices you have made throughout life have not been the best representation of who God has called you to be; and therefore, it leaves you feeling guilty, or in spiritual context, you begin to become convicted by your own life.

If we are going to be more than enough and accept the life that Christ wants us to live, then our decisions are going to have to better represent the God we serve and how He sees us. Not how society categorizes us, not how the world thinks we should do things, and not even what we have been told by people who falsely speak over our lives, but what the Word says about who we are as children of God.

"Being" is a mindset

I can't stress this enough. Everything that God calls us to do as children of God requires us to transform our thinking (Romans 12:2). So if we want to walk into a life that says we are more than enough, we are going to have to let our minds be renewed. We cannot think the same way we used to think. The change has to start with our mind. It even goes back to Proverbs 18:21, the power of our words. Everything we say, hear, and are told takes a seat in our thoughts and ultimately controls how we move in life. Rather we want those things to overtake us or not until we speak over the words of the enemy with the Word of God, we will remain slaves to our own thinking. Philippians 2:5 says, *"Let this mind be in you which was also in Christ Jesus."* Our thinking should align with the thinking of Christ. You need to adapt the mind of Christ in your everyday life but also pertaining to you as an individual.

Maybe you're the same way I was, and you struggle with adapting the mind of Christ toward yourself because you don't really know what His Word has to say about you. Well, maybe these scriptures could help you. God first saw us worthy. We know this because of John 3:16, the scripture of salvation, tells us that God gave His only son to die for us so that we could have eternal life. I'm not sure about you, but I do not know too many people who will die for me. However, Jesus became the sacrifice for our salvation. If that's not love, I don't know what is. The very foundation of our relationship with Christ started with the Father's love toward us because He saw us worthy. Because God loves us, He was willing to sacrifice His only son for our sake. So the first mindset you need to adapt about yourself is that you are *worthy*.

Not only do we find worth in the Word of God, but we also see where God wants *exaltation* for us in Deuteronomy 28:1–14. The first verse in Deuteronomy 28 tells us that if we obey the voice of the Lord and keep His commandments, God will set us high above all nations of the earth. Then the verses to follow proceeds to tell of all the blessing in which God has already said is ours if we just obey. I encourage you to read verses 1–14 in its entirety on your own to get a full view of what God sees for you as a result to your obedience to Him.

The most famous of all these scriptures is found in verse 13. It says that the Lord will make you the head and not the tail. You shall be above only and not be beneath. This is so great because in doing what is right comes exaltation that no man can give nor take away, but it's granted only by the Father. His desire is to set us on high and to bless us because He sees exaltation for us.

Not only does God's Word profess exaltation in His view of us, but it also expresses *purpose* in Jeremiah 29:11, that says, "*'I know the plans I have for you,' declares the Lord, 'plans to prosper you and not to harm you, plans to give you hope and a future.'*" I know some of you, like myself, have heard this scripture many times in your life, but have you ever taken time to really understand what God is saying to us? This scripture echoes the essence of purpose. God is telling us that He has already set up for us to win and to be prosperous before we ever see it for ourselves.

For many of us, we fail to see it for ourselves because we never knew that God saw it for us first. That's why it's so important to consult God's Word about who you are.

God has put inside of each and every last one of us a purpose—a purpose that is far bigger than just our careers, our education, and our daily routine. God has given you a purpose that will bring His name glory and save souls. None of us were placed on this earth with no purpose. If you are struggling to find your purpose, look to God and search what His Word says about who you are and your purpose. Your purpose is the very thing that will lift up God and is specific to your abilities and gifts.

Jeremiah 1:5 says, "*Before I formed you in the womb, I knew you, before you were born I set you apart.*" God's plans and purpose for us have been established since the very beginning. This also means that every route you have taken in your life, God knew you would be there before you ever even arrived, and He still says you are worthy and have a purpose. Embrace the fact that you are meaningful in this world and begin to act like it. We are children of a king, and we are heirs of His kingdom. It's time for us to walk in who we are (Galatians 3:29).

Lifestyle

Live like you are more than enough. We have the Word of God to back us up. This doesn't mean to become arrogant in the way you live, but as children of God, we should never find ourselves doubting what God has placed inside of us or who we are in Him. In order to do this, we have to reject anything that is not a representation of who God says we are. That goes for people, relationships, situations, and even words. Just because you know your worth does not mean that your worth won't experience an attack. The last thing Satan wants is for you to come to a realization of who you really are and establish your worth. Once he sees you're exhibiting a behavior that doesn't keep you enslaved to sinful cycles, he begins to attack. He will send people to speak down on your character. He will present you with temptations that leave you feeling weak. He'll even cause your thoughts to contradict what God already said. But be steadfast (1 Corinthians 15:58). Don't let the trick of the enemy confuse you; the Word of God is true.

So if God says you're worthy, then you are worthy. If God says that you are fearfully and wonderfully made, then you are fearfully and wonderfully made. If God says you are the head and not the tail, then you are the head and not tail. Let God's Word take its place in your heart (Proverbs 3:3; Deuteronomy 11:18). This way, no lie that the enemy speaks over you will be able to override to the Word of God that is written on your heart.

Walk with a purpose because you indeed have a purpose. Each of us are useful in the kingdom of God, but it's up to us to decide whether or not we will work in His kingdom. Someone needs to know that you are not reading this book by coincidence, but yet, there is a word for you in the words you are about to read. Your spirit has been troubled with the act of living for Christ because of the reputation you hold or the things you have done in the past, but I want to tell you that God still wants to use you. God can get more glory out of your mess if you give it over to Him than you could if you continue to hold on to it. God specializes in what seems impossible. God wants you to know that you are not too far gone. In fact, you are never too low where God can't reach you. It is a process, but it's worth the promise. Make the decision today to give your life to God, and allow Him to do a new work in you (2 Corinthians 5:17).

CHAPTER 8

More

These next three chapters are intended to really break down the meaning of this phrase, "more than enough" by breaking down every word in the phrase starting with the first word *more*. The word *more* actually means a greater or an additional amount. Or in my simplified definition, the word *more* simply means excess. Or in my spiritual definition, it means an overflow of what's required. In the title of this book, the word *more* means that limitations have been exceeded and one has acquired too much of something; it implies that what is needed has been exceeded.

So why do we need more than enough? We have just discovered that to have more or more than enough is to have excess. Our reason for needing more than enough is a two-part answer. Psalm 23:5 says, "*You anoint my head with oil and my cup runs over.*" This scripture basically means that the anointing runs over off the vessel (person) and reaches everything close to it. We need more than enough because first, when it runs over, it blesses someone else. The key that you have to understand is that your anointing is not for yourself, but rather, it's for everything and everybody connected to you. What good is an anointing that doesn't help someone else? We don't have a desire to have more than enough so that we can sit on it and brag about it but so that it can run over into someone else's life and bless them as well. Rather it's your children, your coworkers, your neighbor, you grandchildren, or even another church member.

Proverbs 13:22 says, *"A good man leaves an inheritance to his children's children."* You can only leave an inheritance to your children's children if you allow yourself to acquire more than enough and run over for the next generations that come after you. If we really look at Proverbs 13:22, it says an inheritance is left for your children's children. This is significant because it doesn't say for your children but for you grandchildren. And let's be honest, most of us, especially within the African American community, struggle to even obtain college funds for ourselves, not to mention for our children. But the Bible says that we should be so strategic and intentional about how we live our lives that we don't just live for our own comfortability but for that of the next generations to come.

Not only do we need more so that we can run over, but secondly, we need more because as we begin to pour into others, we also begin to lose some for ourselves. So in order to make sure that we never run out, our goal should be to acquire more than enough. In a spiritual concept, it's important for us to remember and know that it is our duty to make sure that we never run out of spiritual authority and anointing. That is why it is so important to keep our relationship with God. That means staying in communication through prayer, being submissive to the Holy Spirit, and being intimate through praise and worship.

More of what?

So what exactly should we as believers have more of? It would be easy for me to list all the things that we want to hear, like money, happiness, love, and so on. I promise you that if you acquire more of what I'm getting ready to explain, all of those other things mentioned will fall in line. The things that God wants us to acquire more than enough of are actually found in Galatians 5:22–23, where the fruit of the spirit are listed. Our overflow should be spiritual; and therefore, we should make it our duty to walk and live in the spirit (Galatians 5:16). Our very desire should be to receive an overflow of love, joy, peace, long-suffering, meekness, goodness, faithfulness, gentleness, and temperance (self-control). This is the fruit that we all should look for in others and the same fruit that we should possess within ourselves.

Matthew 7:16 says, "*You shall know them by their fruit.*" If you want to determine someone's spirituality and relationship with God, check their fruit. Because evidently, one can't say they are close to God and live in the spirit of anger, bitterness, revenge, or jealousy because those are not fruit of the spirit. We should all develop a desire to live in the spirit, possess the fruit of the spirit, and more than enough to last us an entire lifetime. The key is when people see you, your spirit should be the forefront of what they encounter first.

So if we are going to be more than enough and live out loud, we need to embody the fruit of the spirit in our everyday life. One thing to take note of is if we are going to walk in the fruit of the spirit, we must live in the spirit in order to do so. What this means is that, if you don't possess the fruit in your everyday life, it's probably because you are not living in the spirit. To live in the spirit is to die to your emotions and feelings because emotions and feelings are both produced by the flesh. This doesn't mean that you can't be emotional or sensitive or have a soft side. But what this means is that, in situations where your flesh wants to respond with anger, your spirit has to override your flesh and respond with love. When your flesh wants to hasten life because all of your friends are getting married and having kids, your spirit needs to override those emotions with the spirit of long-suffering, which really just means patience.

If we aren't careful, we will let our flesh be the forefront of everything and everyone we encounter in life, and this could cause us to be hateful when God says to love, and it can cause us to live in confusion when God wants us to have peace.

The fruit of the spirit is a very crucial part to a mature Christian's lifestyle. Earlier in this book, I mentioned that our values and our beliefs set us apart from the world, which is true, but what really makes us as believers stand out is when our character is incomparable and we have mastered the art of living in the spirit. You remain humble and meek even after the promotion. You remain reliable and faithful to others even though you've been let down multiple times before. You remain peaceful when others try to provoke you to act out of character. Hear me when I say that it will not be easy to live in the spirit because majority of the time, you don't feel like being loving, but you realize that if you are going to be a representation of Christ, you have to act out of love. You don't necessarily feel like being good to someone who wasn't so good to you, but the Holy Spirit convicts you. You don't feel like living in the spirit, but you have rose to the understanding that your life should be a reflection of Christ; and therefore, if I'm being honest, I don't always want to walk in the fruit of the spirit, but I *have to*.

CHAPTER 9

Than

The word *than* in the phrase, "more than enough," I think is the real game changer and is actually more important than we know. The word *than* implies that something is being compared. In this case, these are the words *more* and *enough*. What I like about this phrase is that the two words that are being compared are opposites and contradict each other. Imagine pouring someone a glass of juice. As long as they say more, you keep pouring. The moment they say enough, you stop pouring. But what if they never say enough, what happens? The cup overflows. This is, in fact, what our lives look like when we say more *than* enough.

I'm really big on words and definitions, so bear with me through this mini English/math lesson. I like the word *than* because the weight it holds is depending on the words that surround it. So the word *than* can either promote or demote depending on the order of the words around it. If we look at the math phrase that says 5 is less than 10, this is a true statement. That in this order, it demotes the number 5 and promotes the number 10. However, if we were to flip this to say 10 is less than 20, also a true statement. But now, instead of the number 10 being promoted, it's now being demoted. Same concept if we were to take the statement and say 5 is greater than 3. In the previous statement, 5 was being demoted, and now in this current statement, it has the role of being promoted.

I wrote all of this to go back to this concept that we established in chapter 1 of this book that tells us that there is power in our words. Though we were talking about numbers in this sense, it's easy to replace those numbers with words that have a negative or positive connotation. For example, Sarah is better than Marie. Same concept, Sarah is somewhere feeling really good about herself and Marie is somewhere trying to figure out what it is that she lacks. Whenever we put the word *than* in between a statement or phrase, it always tells us that a comparison is about to take place.

Anyone who knows me knows how much I despise comparisons. I lived most of my childhood in the shadow of my older siblings. And I remember teachers expecting me to perform the same as my siblings did academically, and I remember the amount of pressure I consumed myself with, trying to meet and exceed those expectations, and it became extremely draining for me. I had to decide who I was going to be, how I would be presented to others, and what they would know me by, and then I vowed to live boldly in whatever that image looked like—even if it didn't represent what had already been established by my older siblings.

When I assess the comparison being declared in the phrase, "more than enough," the two words being compared are *more* and *enough*. I love this comparison because it's saying that what is needed is being exceeded, and you can always make this phrase personal to you by adding a phrase in front of the word *more*. For example, "I have more than enough," "This is more than enough," or "God's love is more than enough." Whatever phrase suits you in whatever season you are in, you can always make it applicable to you in a positive light.

Be careful of thans

As we break down this word *than*, it's important to be mindful that whenever there's a *than*, there's also a comparison. I say be careful of *thans*, with *thans* being symbolic to comparisons. One thing that we have to download into our spirits is that, if we are going to be successful and free from self-inflicted stress, comparisons are a huge no-no. I, myself, am fully human and therefore have been guilty of comparing my life to someone else's. For example, if she can do it, I can't do it, or if my friends are all getting new cars, where's mine? These are the small comparisons that are easy to fall victim to when you are in a place where you don't value the things you already have.

It's easy to look at someone's brand-new car, confused because yours isn't as new as theirs while forgetting that you have a car at all. I solely believe that comparisons are a trick of the enemy to, one, convince you that what you don't have is better than what you do have; and two, to make you take it for granted and fail to acknowledge the blessings that you do have. If the enemy can convince you that the grass is greener on the other side, he can easily throw you off track because instead of focusing and tending to your yard, you were busy coveting someone else's, and now yours hasn't been tended to and it's starting to show.

If you don't take anything else from this book, I want you to know that "more than enough" is not a phrase I'm using to denounce your current blessings, but rather, it is to put you in position of expectancy and not complacency.

I don't want you to hinder yourself from receiving the blessings of God because you're busy worrying about how God is blessing someone else. Truth be told, we sometimes find ourselves coveting things in someone else's life, but if those same things were given to us, they would probably crush us. You're jealous of their car, not knowing the price of their car note. Or you're watching their relationship in awe, not knowing if they're really happy or not.

We as people have mastered the art of making things look good. It's easy to post a cute picture on Instagram and hashtag it with *relationship goals*. It's easy to pull up to work in your nice car every day so everyone can see it. But who's to say that same couple isn't arguing every night? Who's to say that the note of the car isn't becoming too much for them to pay?

We have to be careful of the *thans* or the comparisons in our lives. In fact, the only thing or person that you should be in competition with is the old you. I fight so hard against living in a state of comparison because it's easy to think yourself into a place of depression and even low self-esteem because you sat and thought about what you didn't have, how you don't look, and what you don't do.

As stated before, comparisons are a trick of the enemy to get you off track. So how do you live a life where you don't fall victim to comparisons? Here's my solution. If it is in someone else's possession when you see it, you shouldn't be longing for it. I'm a firm believer of what's mine is mine. I'm not going to have to fight for, toil for it, or wait until someone else is done with it before I can have it. That doesn't mean that everything is going to fall in your lap at once, effortlessly. But it does mean that you won't have to despise someone else for having what you think should be yours. Take it upon yourself to evaluate what you do have and the blessings that already have your name on it, and instead of being upset about what others have, begin to thank God in advance for the blessing that you have yet to see. Because what's yours is yours, and it will have *your* name on it, not someone else's.

CHAPTER 10

Enough

Enough is a very simplistic word but has a very crucial meaning behind it. The word *enough* means as much or as many as required. I have come to find that this word *enough* can actually be problematic because it indicates that there is a limit or a capacity. This book is about doing away with limits and being all that God has called us to be. So I wanted to expound on this word *enough* and explore what makes this word so problematic.

I'm not a big fan of the word *enough* by itself because I often relate its use with negative phrases. If you are anything like me, you have probably heard the phrases, "that's not enough" or "this isn't good enough" or "you aren't good enough." These phrases may sound really good to the issuer of the phrase because they are setting the record that they are looking for more than what has been presented to them. But I find each of these phrases to be problematic because the word *enough* indicates that there is indeed a limit to what they are expecting or looking for. So even though what they received in the past wasn't *enough*, at some point, they are going to come in contact with something or someone who meets their expectations or their limits, and then what?

Limitless

    I want to stick a note here and address the fact that we as believers should never be on a search for *enough*. When God's Word says that He has riches in glory (Philippians 4:19) and all we have to do is ask for it in the name of Jesus and it's ours (John 14:14), at no point should we settle for *enough*. Because we serve a limitless God; therefore, there is no limit to what He can do in our lives.

    I'm standing on faith believing that God is sitting and waiting to see who has the crazy kind of faith that won't leave the presence of God without having received all He has in store for them. The word *enough* means limits, but the phrase, "more than enough" is limitless.

    The truth about limits is that they keep us boxed in and don't give much room to grow. That has never been God's plan for us not to grow. God wants us to grow and expand, but we must do away with the limitations. From this point on, we are vowing, myself included, to never be bound to other people's or our own limitations ever again. Whenever you think a thought that puts limitations on your ability, qualifications, or calling, you have the permission to cast it down and call it unto subjection. Whenever someone speaks something over your life that puts limitations on who you are, you have the permission to speak against it and to tell the enemy to get behind you (Mark 8:33). At the end of the day, that is who we are really at war with—anything that isn't a reflection of God is indeed the enemy. God has given you the permission to speak against every one of his lies.

    I think for most of us, we find ourselves being so distraught about what people have done to us and what they have said to us because we have failed to be able to identify the enemy. This is why discernment is so important because it was never the person, but it was Satan using them. We are too busy waiting for Satan to attack us while looking like Satan. But in fact, Satan knows what is physically appealing and acceptable to all of us; and therefore, he will use those very individuals who look good to us to trap us—the whole time, they're on an assignment by Satan himself. Some of us have connections to friends or boyfriends/girlfriends who may indeed be limiting us from reaching our full potential. We have to identify and discern what's God and what's not, and then we have to strip ourselves from all limitations that leave us only expecting enough.

Enough of enough

If we are going to have enough of anything, let it be enough of enough. Enough of just enough and enough of limitations. Enough of settling for mediocracy and enough of being trapped by the enemy and repeating cycles that keep us enslaved to sin. Because enough is enough. We have to get to a point where we have had enough of not being all that God has called us to be. Enough of being insecure, hurt, bitter, and angry.

Truth be told, you could have read this book in its entirety and still go back to living the same sinful life. It's not until you get to a point where you have had enough of not having more than enough when change will begin to happen. When you get to a place where you are literally fed up with what you have been accepting and how you have been living and not glorifying God, that's when you will begin to live out loud as a child of God. I had to get to a place where I had enough of feeling bad for myself. I had enough of questioning my worth, and I had enough of tolerating less than what I deserved from people who failed to see who I was. I'd had enough, and that is why I wrote this book because I was tired of just enough. I was tired of not feeling like I was enough, and God gave me the words, "more than enough." And I can close out this book by humbly saying, "I am more than enough, I shall have more than enough, and the God I serve is indeed more than enough." This isn't a statement of arrogance because I can't count the number of times I doubted myself, and I can't count the number of times I faced rejections and the hurt of not feeling like I was enough, but God gave me a Word from Him that took away all the pain and replaced it with His peace.

I want to challenge everyone who reads this book to get to a place where you have had enough. It's a time-out for feeling sorry for yourself and having pity parties for all of your setbacks. You can either waddle in your disappointments and stay there, or do something about it and grow from it. But enough is enough. I want you to close this book feeling better about who you are in Christ. Even if your life isn't all the way together, that's okay, but it's up to you to want better for yourself. Your family's lives are depending on it, your children are depending on it, and your marriage is depending on it. If you don't do it for anybody else, do it for them. Make the vow to be all that God has called you to be, and no matter how many times you fall off, keep going. No matter how many times the enemy may try to make you feel worthless, go back to God's Word and stand on what He says about who you are.

It won't be easy and the process won't feel good either, but the promise is worth the process. Sometimes, God has to prune us before He can call us into our full purpose in Christ. There is no such thing as a microwaved anointing. It takes time, and it goes through a process that sometimes hurts. All God is doing is testing to see if you really want what you're believing Him for. Are you really cut out for a life that is more than enough? Allow God to mold you so that you can move out of a life that has you feeling like enough is enough and move into a life that is more than enough.

CONCLUSION

Closing out this book, my prayer is that it helped you as much as it helped me. My prayer is that you were able to find yourself somewhere in the words written and that it has helped you to grasp a better view of what God sees for you. I want you to take the time to really apply what you have read to the areas in your life in which they are most applicable and allow it to transform you. Do not be afraid of the transformation because transformation is only a change—a change that leads to growth. Allow what you have read to grow you into a better person in Christ.

Your words

Take into account everything you have read from the very beginning, and let it have its way in your life. Remember that there is power in your words. Knowing that your words have power, be careful of what you say and how you say it, and ultimately, be careful of who you say it to. Hebrews 13:2 says, "Be not forgetful to entertain strangers: for some have entertained angels unaware." The Message Bible says, "To be hospitable." That means to treat even strangers with respect, being mindful of how you speak and interact with them because you never know who was sent by God. That's why it's so important to be careful not to speak down on individuals without fully knowing who they are.

I want to stress this fact that words do matter. Proverbs says so when it told us that the power of life and death is in our tongue. I'm going to ruin some childhoods, but the saying that goes, "Sticks and stones may break my bones, but words will never hurt me" is a lie. Unfortunately, the right words can hurt. They may not leave visible wounds, but they leave the worse kind of wounds, the ones that are internal and can't be seen. This is why words are so important, and as believers in a world where everyone else says whatever they are feeling, we have to be the ones to speak life and not death into the lives of those we come in contact with.

Don't hesitate to use your words and speak up. Talk about the goodness of God, talk about your testimony, and speak up about your values and who you are. Never allow the enemy to silence you because if he can silence you, he can control you. Keep your voice because there is power in *your* voice, and the enemy knows it. Be bold about everything God has placed on your life and speak on it.

Your faith

Keep your faith no matter what may come your way. Don't give up on God no matter how far He may seem and no matter how hard it may get. We have a Word from heaven that says He will never leave us nor forsake us (Deuteronomy 31:6), and His Word never returns void (Isaiah 55:11). Don't lose your faith. Instead, allow life's circumstances to grow your faith. Believe God to do impossible things in your life. Have a crazy kind of faith that will have other people thinking you're insane. Let your faith shine through situations that seem impossible. Allow your faith to speak the opposite of what you see, so that you always speak life.

Your life

Don't be afraid to stand out. Standing out means you won't fit in. Everyone is not going to like you, everyone won't understand you, and it won't be the most popular decision. You'll even find, as you decide to stand out, that you will lose (fake) friends in the process, but you will gain (real) friends along the way.

As believers, we should live to stand out for God. We are not of the world; therefore, we shouldn't blend in with the world. As believers, we should live and look different from those who are of the world. People should look at your life, without knowing anything about you, and be able to tell that there is something different. If we are going to truly stand out as believers, our relationship with God must be in good standing. A good solid relationship with God above anything else will make it easier to live for God. Evaluate your relationship with God. Are you in constant prayer with God, are you submissive to the Holy Spirit, and are you intimate with God through praise and worship? Those are the three key identifiers to a good relationship with Christ.

What you see

What you see for yourself should align with what God sees for you. God wants you to live a life of overflow; therefore, you should get to a place where you can see more than enough for yourself. Develop self-worth in God's Word. See what God says about your worth and then act accordingly. Make decisions that better represent Christ and continue to grow in how you value yourself. If you don't see value within yourself first, others never will. Find your confidence and esteem in God and begin to live like you are more than enough and like you have blessings of overflow coming your way. Start acting like you are a child of a king. Stop doing things that reflect the old you, and move in a way that edifies your new life in Christ.

Your desires

Evaluate your desires and make sure that they are ordained by God. Consult God before pursuing anything because it will save you a lot of heartache in the long run. Don't confuse your wants with God's desires. Allow God to do a heart change in you by telling your heart what it should desire. Let your desire be to live in God's will and to let Him guide you. Your desire should be, to have, and to be all that God has intended for you. Give your desires to God and let Him do the transformations. Allow purpose to come from God's will for your life so that it benefits more than just you but others around you as well. Don't allow the enemy to trick you into living in your own will based on what you see. Your will is enticing and tempting. God's will is simplistic and not flashy. Choose God's will.

Who you decide to be

Remember that the state of being starts with your mind. You have to decide who you want to be before you can be it. If you are going to be more than enough, you have to first think like you are more than enough. More than enough isn't just a saying, but rather, it's a lifestyle. You have to make the decision to live a more than enough lifestyle in every area of your life. People should see the overflow you are living in everywhere you go. When making the decision to be more than enough, it's important to take into consideration what God says about who we are and how He sees us according to His Word. He sees us as worthy, exalted, and purposeful according to John 3:16, Deuteronomy

28:1–14, and Jeremiah 29:11. Your goal should be to prove God's Word right about who you are by walking in what His Word says.

Live for more

More means excess or overflow. Our reason for wanting more goes far beyond ourselves. Our overflow is for everyone else connected to us. It is our anointing that we need to run over. We also need overflow because as we pour into others, we begin to lose some of what we had, so we should be receiving a constant outpour of God's anointing so that we never run out. We shouldn't just live in expectancy of more anointing but for more spiritual stamina to walk in the fruit of the spirt as well.

It's the Holy Spirit who helps us live in the spirit. Your spirit man should be the forefront of what people see when they come in contact with you. To live in the spirit is to crucify your flesh. We are in a spiritual fight to kill our flesh every day. It won't be easy, but it gets easier as you allow yourself to overflow with the fruit of the spirit. You will find yourself responding to things God's way without even having to think too hard because as you live in the spirit, you are allowing the Holy Spirit to do away with all the things that don't represent Him.

The thans *in your life*

Remember that the word *than* indicates that there is a comparison taking place. We have to remember to be careful not to be consumed by comparisons. As stated in chapter 9, comparisons are a trick of the enemy. Comparisons come to do two things. The first is to make you think that what you don't have is better than what you do have. The second is to make you forget or take for granted what you do have because it doesn't look like the thing you don't have.

This is indeed how the enemy can make you look foolish and get you out of alignment with God's will when you begin to hunger after what is not yours while failing to maintain what is yours. Don't allow comparisons to trick you or confuse you. Be grateful and remain prayerful for God will reveal to you what's yours and what's not.

Have you had enough?

The word *enough* is a word of limitations. The name of this book is called *More Than Enough*, which is a phrase that does away with all limitations. We should never walk around life asking for or wanting enough of anything simply because we serve a limitless God; therefore, our desires should be to live an abundant life. The only things we should have had enough of is the cycles that keep us far from God and the feelings that keep us engulfed in sin. Every individual needs to get to that place where enough is enough. You have had enough of living from paycheck to paycheck, enough of searching for happiness in people, enough of not loving yourself in spite of your flaws, and enough of falling as victim to the enemies' traps. I declare that God's children will rise up and declare that they have had enough of being powerless and will begin to do whatever it takes to fight against the wiles of the enemy in order to live the abundant life that God has called for all of us to live.

My push against the word *enough* is not to awaken a spirit of greed and ungratefulness but rather to push you out of a place of complacency and into a place of expectancy. More than enough is the push that I needed to be able to see in myself what God already saw in me. And I don't think I'm the only one. The phrase, "more than enough" is not a phrase of arrogance or haughtiness, but for me, it came from a place of confusion, insecurities, and rejection. It's from that very place that my life changed. I discovered a new testimony, and I'm able to share what helped me with other people all over the world.

As I finally bring this book to a close, I leave you with the words that picked me up out of some of my lowest places in life. I want you to know personally that no matter where you may be in life and no matter how far you may feel from God, *you* are *more than enough*. All you have to do is tap into the life that God has waiting for you by choosing to live for and serve God. It's time to start living like you are more than enough. There are so many blessings and an anointing with your name on it waiting for you if you would just come to know who you are in Christ and walk in the truth that is the Word of God. There is a new blessed life calling your name.

I'm going to be honest, it is going to cost you some things and people you thought you needed, but God will reveal to you who you really need to make your walk with Christ successful. If you have read this and know Christ and you have already been saved, I challenge you to make that unpopular decision to live out loud for Christ and watch what He does in your life. I did it, and I couldn't be happier. If you're reading this and you aren't saved, I challenge you to try out the God that has been so gracious to me and to other people that I know. I want you to take the first steps to draw closer to God, whatever that looks like for you. Ask God to guide you to the right people and the right pastor, and even if you fall off, don't let it deter you. Keep going because I promise you, you won't regret it. Take the steps toward salvation, and let God do the rest. Don't forfeit a life of abundance by holding on to what you have become so comfortable with, allow God to change you so that you can grow, and live a life that is more than enough.

DISCUSSION QUESTIONS

Chapter 1: There Is Power in Your Words

1. What makes our words powerful?
2. How should we as Christians speak?
3. How can we as Christians speak life into our situations?
4. Have you ever had words spoken to you that hurt you? Have you forgiven that individual?
5. Have you ever spoken words to someone that may have hurt them?

Chapter 2: Speak Up!

1. What are some positive things you can speak up about?
2. What are some ways you can speak up about your values?
3. What are some ways you can speak up about what you believe in?
4. Why is it important for us as believers to have values?
5. Do you have any dreams/visions for your life that were given to you by God? What are they?

Chapter 3: Have Faith

1. Why is faith so important as a believer?
2. How can your faith win souls?

3. What is the difference between believing God and believing in God?
4. What is faith?
5. Why do we as humans tend to struggle so much with having faith?

Chapter 4: Stand Out

1. What does it mean to be doers of God's Word? How can we be doers of His Word?
2. What message can we take from Revelations 3:16?
3. When we partake in worldly behaviors, who are we claiming to serve?
4. According to Matthew 6:24, why is it impossible to serve two masters?
5. What are some ways we can be about God's business?
6. What are the three keys necessary to have a good relationship with God?
7. Discuss the meaning of John 12:32.

Chapter 5: See It

1. What are some ways or things we can do to help us see more than enough for ourselves?
2. What about us has to change or be renewed so that we can see more than enough for ourselves?
3. How do we know that God sees us as worthy?
4. What are some ways we can do better in our walk with Christ?
5. What are some ways we can reject less in our own lives?

Chapter 6: Desire It

1. What is the prerequisite before God can give us our heart's desires?
2. What does God mean when He says He will give us our heart's desires?
3. What are desires?
4. What are wants?
5. What are some differences between self-will and God's will?
6. What should our posture look like in seasons where God wants us to wait?

Chapter 7: Be It

1. Where do we develop self-worth?
2. How does our mind/thinking help us to *be more than enough*?
3. What should we do to make sure that we don't become slaves to our own thinking?
4. What are the three things God sees for us (Deuteronomy 28:1–14; John 3:16; Jeremiah 29:11)?
5. What does it mean to live like we are more than enough?
6. What are some ways you can live like you are more than enough?

Chapter 8: More

1. What is "more"?
2. What are the two reasons as to why we need more than enough?
3. What do we need more of?
4. What is the fruit of the spirit?
5. How do we live in the spirit/the fruit of the spirit?
6. What are some things you can do daily to help you respond in the spirit and not in the flesh?

Chapter 9: Than

1. What word is the word *than* symbolic to?
2. Why are comparisons a huge no-no?
3. What two ways does the enemy use comparisons to trick us?
4. What ends up happening to your yard when you allow the enemy to convince you that the grass is greener somewhere else?
5. What is the author's purpose for the phrase, "more than enough"?

Chapter 10: Enough

1. What does the word *enough* mean?
2. Why is the word *enough* problematic?
3. Why shouldn't we as believers be on a search for enough?
4. What is the truth about limits?
5. What are some things that we as believers need to say enough to?
6. What are some things in your life that you need to say enough to?

ABOUT THE AUTHOR

April Williams is an educator, a youth leader, and an ambassador for God. April was born in Detroit, Michigan, and later moved to Kalamazoo, Michigan, where she attended Western Michigan University to pursue a degree in English. Upon graduating, she began working at an elementary school as a paraprofessional as she continued to answer the call of God on her life.

April is a dedicated and loving sister, daughter, friend, and servant of Christ. She made it her duty at a young age to put God first and to live for Christ regardless of what others thought. April's desire is to continue to allow God to use her life to reach the lives of those around her. April aspires to continue to use her influence to help youth in the education field and throughout the world by doing what she was called to do—lead.